Suddenly, Aladdin's father died. Seeing that her son was idle and would never become a tailor like his father, Aladdin's mother sold the shop and started spinning cotton so as to make enough money for herself and her son. But, even after his father's death, Aladdin did nothing to improve his ways and help his poor mother.

One day, while Aladdin was playing in the street, a strange-looking man came up to him. This man was a sorcerer and had special powers of magic. For long years he had been searching for a boy who looked exactly like Aladdin. "This is just the boy I need for my plans," he told himself. "After so many years of wandering through the countries of the world since leaving my home country of Morocco, I have at last found him."

After learning everything about Aladdin from people in the street, the Moroccan sorcerer went up to the boy and asked him if he was perhaps the son of so-and-so the tailor.

"Yes indeed," answered Aladdin, "but my father is now dead."

At these words, tears began to run down the bearded face of the man from Morocco.

"Do not tell me," he said in a broken voice, "that my one and only brother is dead!"

"Are you his brother?" asked Aladdin in astonishment.

"Of course," said the man, "and I have been travelling all these years in order that I might once again see his face." The man went on weeping for some time, then he wiped away the tears and his face broke into a wide smile.

"But as soon as I saw you," said the Moroccan, "I knew that you were his son. Now it is as if I have a son of my own."

With these words the man embraced Aladdin and kissed him on both cheeks.

"And do you now live with your mother?" the man asked Aladdin.

Aladdin nodded and the Moroccan gave him ten gold coins and told him to go and give them to his mother. "Tell her," he said to Aladdin, "that the brother of your father has come to the city and would like to have supper with you both tomorrow night."

Aladdin had never seen so much money in all his life. Immediately, he ran off to tell his mother the good news about this relative of theirs who had suddenly appeared in the city. But although Aladdin's mother was pleased to receive such a large sum of money, she told her son that clearly there was some mistake as her husband had never mentioned a brother.

The next evening the Moroccan sorcerer, dressed in a long gown, a large turban and bright yellow pointed slippers, knocked at the door of the house. He brought with him a large basket of fruit and pastries for their supper. He told Aladdin's mother how he had searched all over the world for the brother he had not seen for so many years. He then talked so lovingly about his dear brother that Aladdin's mother began to believe that this man, who spoke with such a strange accent, was really the brother of her dead husband.

ALADDIN
AND THE LAMP

Retold by Denys Johnson-Davies
Illustrations by Walid Taher

Aladdin was the only son of a tailor who lived far away in the land of China. His father had tried to teach him some skills with a needle and scissors but Aladdin was not a serious boy. He preferred to spend his time with his young friends, so whenever his father's back was turned Aladdin would run out of the shop to play in the streets.

After supper, as they sat drinking glasses of tea and eating the pastries he had brought, the man explained that in his home city in Morocco he was a wealthy merchant. He had made a sudden decision to search for his brother, for he had no other relatives and did not wish to die without seeing him again. Eventually, he had come to China and, with the help of God Almighty, had been wandering in the streets of the city when he had come across Aladdin.

"I knew at once," said the man, "that this young lad was the son of my brother."

He then asked Aladdin: "And what trade are you learning, my son?"

Aladdin kept silent and looked down at the floor.

"I am sorry to tell you," said the mother, "that my son spends his days playing in the streets and does nothing to help his poor old mother."

The Moroccan put his hand on Aladdin's shoulder. "Perhaps he does not want to learn a trade," he said. "Perhaps it would be better for him to become a merchant like myself. He could sit in a shop and talk to customers who come and buy from him. I can help him to start a business."

Of course Aladdin was delighted at the idea of having a shop and entertaining all his friends. His mother, too, could not believe her good luck.

The next morning the Moroccan came to the house and took Aladdin to a tailor's shop where he bought him a fine robe. Then the man suggested that the two of them take a walk outside the city. They walked for hour after hour until Aladdin was exhausted, though the Moroccan seemed as fresh as ever. When they were out in the open countryside, the Moroccan came to a stop under a high mountain. This was the place which, ever since he had left his home town in Morocco, the sorcerer had known about. This was the place where, with Aladdin's help, he would find what he was searching for.

"Sit down and rest for a while," the sorcerer told Aladdin. "Soon I shall show you things that the eye of man has never seen before."

When Aladdin had rested, the sorcerer told him to look around in the desert for some sticks to make a fire. Then, when the fire was alight, the Moroccan opened a little box made of olive wood from which he took some incense. He threw some of the incense into the flames, as he spoke some magic words in a strange language. Suddenly the sky became dark with clouds and the ground shook, then a great hole opened in front of them. Aladdin looked down at his feet and saw a large block of marble with a copper handle.

Aladdin was so terrified that he tried to run away, but the sorcerer gave him a blow to the side of his head which knocked him senseless. When Aladdin had recovered, the man said to him: "That was to teach you to obey me, my son. If you do as I tell you, you will become richer than a king. And to help you, here is a ring to keep you safe. Its genie is a genie of travel."

The sorcerer took a plain silver ring from his finger and gave it to Aladdin.

"Tell me what to do, uncle," said Aladdin quietly, putting the ring on his finger.

"Only you can lift the stone and discover what lies beneath it," said the man. "Pull the copper handle and say aloud your name and the names of your father and mother."

The sorcerer knew that he could never get what he wanted without Aladdin's help. It was only Aladdin who could help him to complete the circle, and he had come all this way to China to find him.

"But it's far too heavy for me," said Aladdin as he took hold of the copper handle.

"Say the words, as I told you," said the sorcerer, "and it will be easy." So Aladdin said his own name and those of his mother and father, and then pulled. He was surprised to feel the marble moving. Under it he saw a long staircase that went down to a great cave.

"Go into the cave," said the sorcerer to Aladdin. "At the bottom of the stairs you will find four rooms, two on each side. In each room you will see open chests full of gold and silver. Do not stop for a moment and do not touch those pieces of gold and silver, or you will immediately be turned into a piece of black stone! Walk on and you will find yourself in front of a heavy metal door. Push it open and you will enter a beautiful garden with many fruit trees. Hanging from the branches you will find fruits of many colours. Do not try to pick any of these! When you have passed under these trees you will come to more stairs; at the top of them you will find a lamp hanging from the ceiling. Take the lamp and come back as quickly as you can."

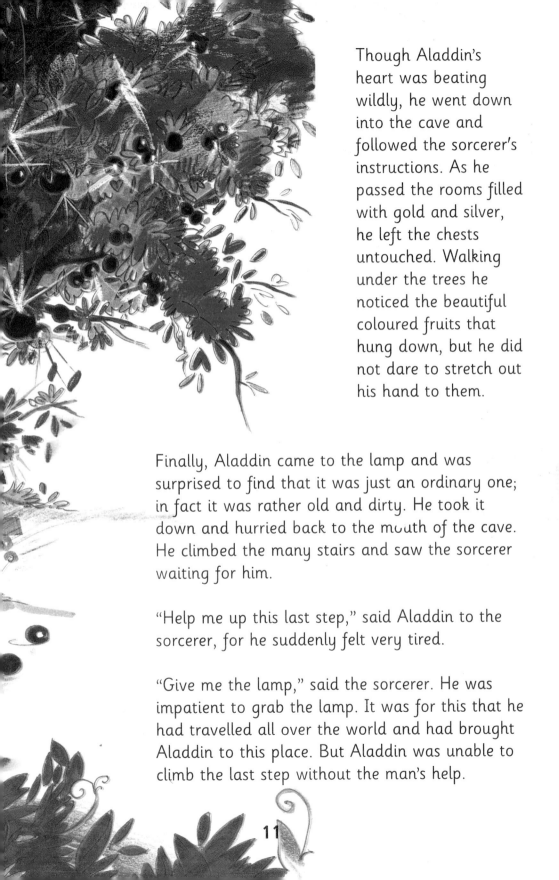

Though Aladdin's heart was beating wildly, he went down into the cave and followed the sorcerer's instructions. As he passed the rooms filled with gold and silver, he left the chests untouched. Walking under the trees he noticed the beautiful coloured fruits that hung down, but he did not dare to stretch out his hand to them.

Finally, Aladdin came to the lamp and was surprised to find that it was just an ordinary one; in fact it was rather old and dirty. He took it down and hurried back to the mouth of the cave. He climbed the many stairs and saw the sorcerer waiting for him.

"Help me up this last step," said Aladdin to the sorcerer, for he suddenly felt very tired.

"Give me the lamp," said the sorcerer. He was impatient to grab the lamp. It was for this that he had travelled all over the world and had brought Aladdin to this place. But Aladdin was unable to climb the last step without the man's help.

11

"Hold out your hand and pull me up," Aladdin asked. But when the Moroccan tried to snatch the lamp from Aladdin's hand, Aladdin quickly swung the lamp away.

The sorcerer went mad with anger. He turned to the fire which was blazing behind him and threw some more incense into it, calling out magic words.

Immediately the earth closed up and Aladdin found himself a prisoner in the cave. He now understood that the wicked Moroccan was not his uncle at all and that he had played a trick on Aladdin. But why, Aladdin asked himself, had this man gone to so much trouble just for an old lamp?

Aladdin was unable to tell how long he spent in the cave. Certainly it was many hours, or even days. Gradually he became hungrier and thirstier. How long could someone live without food or water? He searched the cave, looking in all the different rooms that held so much treasure, but found nothing to eat. Then he remembered the fruit he had seen on the trees.

But he was disappointed to find that the fruits of many brilliant colours were in fact pieces of glass. They were pretty and sparkled brightly, so he picked some and put them in his pockets.

Then he went back to the entrance to the cave, where he had left the lamp. He sat down on the ground. He was in despair at the thought that he could find no way out of the cave, and that he would soon die of starvation. As he sat with his back to the wall of the cave, he raised his hands to his face as though about to say a prayer. He noticed the ring that the sorceror had given him and he remembered the sorceror's words: "Its genie is a genie of travel." What had the sorceror meant by those words?

Aladdin took the ring from his finger and rubbed it. Immediately, in a puff of smoke, a tall, dark genie appeared.

"I am the servant of the owner of the ring," said the genie in a loud, crackling voice. "Command me to do what you want."

"Take me and all the contents of this cave to my mother's house," said Aladdin, though he did not really believe that this would happen.

"That is not in my power," answered the genie. "Unlike some other genies, I can only take you - and you alone - from one place to another."

"Then take me to my home in the city," said Aladdin.

"I hear and I obey," said the genie with a smile, "but do not forget your lamp!"

Aladdin would have forgotten all about the lamp if the genie had not reminded him. "I suppose I might as well take it," said Aladdin to himself.

The next second, Aladdin found himself lying on his back, with his mother sprinkling water over his face. He saw that he was safely back home. "Mother, I'm starving," he said to her. "Please bring me some food - anything!"

His mother brought him some cold beans and rice, which was all she had in the house. "You've been away for days," she told him. "Where have you been and where's your uncle?"

While he was eating, Aladdin told his mother about his adventures with the Moroccan sorcerer.

She shook her head and said: "I knew from the beginning that he was no uncle of yours, that he was nothing but a cheat. Thank God, my son, that you've escaped."

Aladdin was so tired that he was soon fast asleep. When he awoke the following day, he again felt hungry, but there was no food in the house. As he lay with an empty feeling in his stomach, he remembered the lamp he had brought from the cave.

"Bring me the lamp, mother. I shall go and sell it and buy some food."

Aladdin's mother saw that the lamp was dirty, so she took it to the kitchen and decided to give it a good clean. Then, as she rubbed the lamp with a cloth, she was terrified by a great genie with staring eyes, who had popped out of the lamp in a cloud of smoke.

"I am your slave," the genie told her. "Just tell me what you want and it shall be done."

Hearing voices, Aladdin quickly ran to the kitchen and took the lamp from his mother's hands. He had already seen a genie, so this one did not frighten him.

"Slave of the lamp," he told the genie. "We are hungry, so please bring us some food."

The genie brought so much food that Aladdin and his mother ate from it for several days. When the food was finished Aladdin again rubbed the lamp and ordered another tray of food. Seeing also that the tray was made of solid silver, Aladdin found that he was able to sell it in the market for a good price. And so, from the regular sale of the silver trays, he and his mother were never hungry. There was even money left over for each of them to buy some new clothes, and they gave away to the poor the clothes they had been wearing before.

During these days, Aladdin began to explore the alleys of the city and its markets. At the same time he watched the merchants and learned how to bargain with them when he went to sell his silver trays. He also began to look at the gold and silver shops and the shops which sold precious stones. It was not long before he realised that the stones he had taken from the cave were not just pieces of coloured glass - they were magnificent rubies and emeralds and other jewels. Though he knew that the jewels he had would make him rich, he saw no reason to sell any of them, for he was not greedy - and did not he and his mother have the very best food, brought to them regularly by the genie?

One morning, as he was wandering around the markets of the city, he heard a man from the palace calling out in the street. He was ordering everyone to close their shops and go into their houses because the Sultan's daughter, the beautiful Badr al-Budour, was on her way to the city's baths and nobody must see her.

Like everyone else, Aladdin had heard how lovely the Sultan's daughter was. He was determined to see her, so he hid himself behind

19

a doorway just by the entrance to the baths. As the princess entered she lifted her veil for a moment and he caught sight of her lovely face that was like the full moon - just like her name, which means "full moon" in Arabic.

From that moment Aladdin became a prisoner to his love for this beautiful princess. He returned home, but found he had no appetite for the food his mother placed in front of him. Thinking he must be ill, his mother suggested calling a doctor, so Aladdin was forced to tell her how he had seen the princess and fallen in love with her.

His mother was very unhappy to hear this news, for what hope was there for the simple son of a tailor to marry the daughter of the Sultan?

"I am determined to ask for her hand," insisted Aladdin.

"Don't be so foolish!" said his mother in horror. "You will only bring unhappiness to both of us."

In the end Aladdin was able to persuade his mother to go to the palace and try to see the Sultan.

"But I cannot go there," his mother protested, "without taking a present for the Sultan."

"Don't worry, mother," Aladdin said to her. "I shall give you a present for him which will amaze him."

Aladdin, for the first time, showed her the magnificent jewels he had taken from the trees in the cave. She stared at them, unable to believe their beauty and size.

Of course, at the palace no-one paid any attention to the woman who was standing timidly by the door. At last, when the room was almost empty, the Sultan noticed her and said to his minister: "Who is that woman standing over there? She has been here since the morning. See what she wants."

The minister took Aladdin's mother towards the Sultan's throne. Her knees were trembling so much that she could hardly walk. When she stood before the Sultan she bowed down and kissed the ground. Only with difficulty did she find the courage to tell the Sultan how her son had caught a glimpse of the princess and had fallen in love with her.

"He would like to make her his wife." she added. She was pleased to find that the Sultan did not show any anger at her words; instead, he leaned back in his throne and laughed.

"He has asked me to bring Your Majesty a present," said Aladdin's mother, looking up at the Sultan, and she untied the cloth in which she and Aladdin had wrapped some of the jewels.

"What have you got there?" asked the Sultan. He stared in wonder at the jewels whose brilliance lit up the far corners of the room.

"I have never seen such jewels!" he cried. "Among all my treasures there is not a single stone to compare with any of these."

"They are yours, Your Majesty - a present from my son Aladdin."

The Sultan thanked Aladdin's mother and said that he would like to meet her son.

"Ask him to honour us with his presence at the palace tomorrow morning," said the Sultan.

 laddin was delighted when he heard how his mother had been received at the court, and how the Sultan had accepted the gift of jewels. He put on his best robe, the one that the sorcerer had bought him, and was taken to the Sultan's throne by the minister. However, this minister had been hoping that Badr al-Budour, the princess, would one day become the wife of his own son. The minister advised the Sultan to be careful about young Aladdin.

"We have made enquiries, Your Majesty," said the minister, "and we have found that Aladdin's father was nothing but a tailor. We cannot understand how he owns the kind of jewels that he presented to Your Majesty."

"Let us judge the young man when we see him," said the Sultan.

The Sultan was very impressed by Aladdin and the two of them sat talking for some time. Aladdin mentioned to the Sultan that he wanted to marry Badr al-Budour and assured him that he was a rich man and able to keep the princess in luxury.

So the next day Aladdin sent his mother once again to the palace with another present of magnificent jewels. In the meantime, though, the minister had been talking to the Sultan and had tried to persuade him not to allow his daughter to marry Aladdin.

"Demand such a high price for your daughter that will show us whether this son of a tailor really is rich," suggested the minister.

When Aladdin's mother again appeared in front of the Sultan to ask for the hand of the princess, the Sultan said to her:

"Go to your son and tell him that I am a powerful and wealthy ruler and that the price for my daughter's hand is therefore a high one. What I want from your son is for him to bring forty dishes of pure gold; all these dishes must be filled with jewels like the ones he has already presented to me. These dishes must be carried by forty slaves through the streets of the city to my palace. Only then shall Badr al-Budour become your son's wife."

Aladdin's mother returned home in despair. What could she tell her son? How could she let him know that the Sultan had made it impossible for him ever to win the hand of the princess?

Aladdin was waiting for his mother, eager for her news.

"My son," she told him, "you must give up all hope. We are simple people and it was foolish of you to think that you could marry the Sultan's daughter."

She then told Aladdin of the price the Sultan had demanded for the hand of his daughter.

When Aladdin and his mother went to look at the jewels that were left they found that there were not enough to fill one dish, and certainly not enough to pay for forty slaves to carry the dishes.

Aladdin thought for a while, then shouted: "I forgot all about the lamp! If the genie can bring us our food, perhaps he can bring dishes of gold with jewels, and also forty slaves."

So Aladdin took out the lamp and rubbed it. He explained to the genie that until now he had always asked for food which the genie had brought on silver dishes.

"But this time," said Aladdin, "I want forty dishes of gold, all filled with jewels and I want them to be carried by forty slaves."

All the genie said was: "I hear and I obey," and a few seconds later forty slaves came walking into the house carrying gold dishes filled with jewels.

What a wonderful sight it was! Aladdin's mother walked through the streets of the city in front of forty slaves carrying the dishes, all dressed in magnificent robes.

The Sultan was amazed at how quickly Aladdin had brought the gifts he had demanded. He turned to his minister and said: "Does this not show you how mistaken you have been about this young man?"

The minister bowed his head and had to admit that he had never seen anything so remarkable, but his heart was still full of hate for this son of a tailor.

The Sultan then spoke to Aladdin's mother: "Go to your son and tell him that his gift is accepted and that we will hold the wedding party tonight. Tonight the princess Badr al-Budour shall be married to Aladdin."

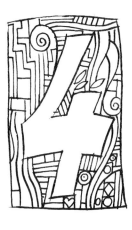

Aladdin was overjoyed when his mother returned home and told him that the Sultan had agreed and that the wedding would take place that night.

Once again, Aladdin had to ask for help from the genie of the lamp, for of course he did not have the proper clothes in which to be married to a princess.

"Bring me a robe more splendid than anything ever worn by any prince at his wedding," Aladdin ordered the genie. Then, after taking a bath, he put on the new robe and perfumed himself. As this son of a poor tailor looked at himself in the mirror, he said: "Glory be to God who changes others and remains Himself unchanged!"

Again Aladdin rubbed the lamp, and said: "Bring me a fine Arabian horse and two dozen horsemen to ride in front of me and two dozen behind me, all dressed in splendid clothes and carrying swords and spears that will shine in the sunlight."

Long tables had been laid out for the wedding feast, with every kind of delicious food. All the noblemen from the city were invited, while rulers and princesses from neighbouring countries filled the great halls of the palace. In a seat of honour sat Aladdin's mother, dressed in expensive robes and looking like a queen, with a smile of happiness on her face.

The feast went on long into the night, and when all was finished Aladdin and his bride went off to a wing of the palace where the Sultan had prepared special rooms for them.

Aladdin, though, wanted his bride to have her own palace, a palace even more splendid than that of the Sultan.

"If Your Majesty would be kind enough to give me some land nearby," Aladdin asked the Sultan, "I shall build a palace for myself and the princess."

"That will take many months," said the Sultan, "but of course you may have whatever land you wish. Why do you not build on that great space that lies directly in front of my own palace?"

Aladdin answered the Sultan that he would build his palace more quickly than anyone had ever done before, and the Sultan and his minister exchanged looks of disbelief.

As soon as he was alone, Aladdin rubbed the lamp and called the genie.

"I have a big and difficult job for you," said Aladdin. "I have told the Sultan that I want a palace to be built and that he will be astonished at how quickly it is finished. Is it possible to do this by the morning?"

"There is nothing that is not possible," answered the genie.

"And one more thing," said Aladdin. "I would like to have a rich red carpet decorated with gold thread, connecting the Sultan's palace and my palace, so that I may take my bride along it to her new home."

When the Sultan awoke the next morning, he looked through the window and was amazed to find a splendid palace facing his own, and connected to his palace by a magnificent length of carpet.

The minister was almost speechless with wonder, but also with envy.

"The only way he could have done this is through magic," he said to the Sultan.

Later that day Aladdin left the Sultan and, with Badr al-Budour sitting behind him on his horse, he rode down the red carpet to the newly built palace. As he rode he threw money to the citizens of the city who had gathered to watch him and his bride.

What had the wicked Moroccan sorcerer been doing while all this was happening? He had left Aladdin to die in the cave, thinking that one day he would go back to it and find a way in to get the magic lamp.

One day, after he had returned to his home in faraway Morocco, the sorcerer had made magic patterns in the sand in order to make sure that Aladdin had really died in the cave. But in the pictures that came out of the patterns, he saw no sign of either Aladdin or the lamp. What had happened to the boy and where was the lamp?

Later, he again drew magic pictures in the sand. This time he saw that Aladdin was now a man of great riches and that he was living in a palace and was married to the Sultan's daughter. And there, hanging on the wall in Aladdin's palace, he saw the magic lamp.

The sorcerer was filled with rage and a desire for revenge. He decided to travel once again to where Aladdin was living. Finally, after a long voyage full of difficulties and dangers - for the wicked sorcerer had no magic lamp or ring to help him - he arrived at the city in China.

He walked through the streets of the city and heard many stories about Aladdin and his great wealth, about the beauty of his wife, and the size of the palace in which they lived. The sorcerer grew angrier and angrier that Aladdin had won all this with the lamp. He knew that the most important thing was somehow to steal the lamp from Aladdin. But how could he ever make his way into the palace?

He then thought of a plan by which he could get the lamp. In one of the alleys of the city he found a coppersmith. "Make me some fine copper lamps," the sorcerer said to him. "Make them with great speed and I shall reward you well for them."

The next day, when the lamps were ready, the sorcerer went to the shop and paid the man his price. He then took the lamps and put them in a basket which he carried at his side. He wandered through the streets of the city, calling out at the top of his voice: "New lamps for old! New lamps for old!"

Of course, people laughed at him, thinking he was mad to give a bright new lamp in exchange for some old one that probably did not work. But the sorcerer paid no attention to what they were saying and called out even louder as he approached the palace where Aladdin and the princess lived. "New lamps for old! New lamps for old!"

Badr al-Budour's maid ran to the window and looked down.

"What a funny old man!" she thought. "Why should he exchange a new lamp for an old one?"

Then she remembered that they too, in the palace, had an old lamp, one that the master himself had brought with him. She went to get it and ran down to the street.

The sorcerer quickly gave her one of his new lamps and hurried off through the alleys with the magic lamp hidden under his robe. He went immediately to the desert that surrounded the city and there, when he was sure that no-one was watching him, he took out the lamp and rubbed it.

"I am at your command," said the genie, appearing before him.

The sorcerer gave an evil smile as he told the genie: "Pick up Aladdin's palace and all that is in it, and put it down in the city in which I live in Morocco - and take me as well."

In an instant, the wicked sorcerer, the beautiful palace and all its luxurious furniture were transported to Morocco, where they suddenly appeared in one of that country's lovely gardens.

Now that the Moroccan sorcerer had the lamp, with its power to bring anything that its owner wanted, he was a happy man.

6

When, the next morning, the Sultan woke up and looked through the window of his bedroom, he was astonished to find that Aladdin's palace was no longer there. How could such a building have vanished? The Sultan called for his minister and asked him to look out of the window.

"What do you see?" asked the Sultan. The minister looked at the empty ground where the palace had been.

"Nothing, Your Majesty," said the minister.

"Exactly!" said the Sultan in a rage. "In the same way as it was built overnight, so it has disappeared overnight."

"I have always told Your Majesty that this young man Aladdin was nothing but a cheap magician. Perhaps he made us imagine that there was a palace there."

"Well, there's no palace there now," said the Sultan angrily. "And what I'd like to know is where Aladdin is now. And where, too, is my daughter?"

"Aladdin, Your Majesty, has gone out hunting," answered the minister. "As for Badr al-Budour, she seems to have disappeared with the palace."

"Arrest Aladdin immediately and bring him here in chains," ordered the Sultan. "He will pay for this with his head!"

A number of officers and men were ordered to go out into the desert and search for Aladdin and his party of hunters. When Aladdin was dragged in chains through the city streets, the citizens were sad. They loved and admired him and were angry when they heard that the Sultan was planning to have him beheaded.

When Aladdin was brought before the Sultan, he tried to speak and to find out what had happened; but the Sultan would not listen.

"Behead this magician!" ordered the Sultan. The executioner spread the leather mat and made Aladdin kneel on it, with his head forward and his hands tied behind his back.

But the news that Aladdin was going to be beheaded had spread through the city. Just as the sword was about to fall on Aladdin's neck, the minister rushed into the room and told the Sultan that the people were at the palace gates. They were even planning to attack the palace itself.

"The people are threatening our lives!" cried the minister. "Give Aladdin his life, Your Majesty, even though we all know that he deserves to die a thousand deaths."

"What has happened to your palace?" shouted the Sultan at Aladdin. "Where is my daughter?"

"Your daughter? My wife?" cried Aladdin. "Has she too disappeared?"

"Don't you know?" said the Sultan. "I am giving you your life only so that you may find my daughter and explain to me what has happened to that palace. I give you twenty-four hours to do this. If not, I swear by this white beard of mine, that you will lose your head."

Though Aladdin was still alive, he had no idea what to do. Where was the palace? And where was his lovely wife? And where, too, was the magic lamp? From where could he start, with no money and no-one to help him? He went outside the city walls, carrying with him a bag of food which a kind grocer had given to him. He sat down by a small stream and decided to pray before having something to eat, for he had not eaten since early morning.

He started to wash himself in the stream before praying and took some water in the palms of his hands. As he was doing this, he saw the ring on his finger. It was the magic ring he had been given by the wicked sorcerer so long ago, the same ring that had helped him to escape from the cave. He had forgotten all about it during this time, for, with the lamp, he had had no need of it.

He took off the ring and rubbed it. Immediately the genie appeared in front of him.

"I am at your command, master," said the genie.

"You said you have the power to take me anywhere I wish," said Aladdin.

"That is correct," replied the genie. "But, in exchange, I beg you to return the ring to me. In this way you will give me my freedom."

"O genie of the ring, I ask you to take me to my palace which was once in this city, wherever it may be. Now take back the ring," and Aladdin took it off and placed it in the palm of the genie's hand.

In a flash the genie took the ring and transported Aladdin to the far corner of Africa, where the palace now stood. Aladdin found himself lying in the shade of a tree right under the window of his princess, Badr al-Budour. At that moment, like so many things in this life that happen by chance, one of

the princess's maids looked down from the window and saw her master. Quickly she went to Badr al-Budour to give her the good news.

The maid hurried down to let Aladdin into the palace by a secret door, and soon Aladdin and Badr al-Budour were together again.

"Tell me," Aladdin said to her, "how you were brought here with the palace."

Badr al-Budour told him about the old lamp which the maid had exchanged for the new one.

"The wicked sorcerer," the princess continued, "told me that my father had had your head cut off and that I was now free to marry him. He pretends to be in love with me."

"He is the most wicked man alive," Aladdin told her, "and as long as he has the lamp we are powerless against him.

But where is the lamp now?"

"He always carries it with him," said the princess.

Aladdin thought for a while, then said to Badr al-Budour: "I shall leave you now and return at night. I have a plan for putting an end to this man."

Aladdin left the palace by the secret door and wandered round this strange foreign city which was surrounded by palm trees and over which hung the snow-covered mountains of Africa. It was also a city famous for its bazaars and little shops and stalls that sold perfumes and magic medicines.

At one of these stalls he stopped and bought a small bottle of liquid, without taste or colour, that would put anyone who drank from it into a deep sleep. Aladdin then returned to the palace, entering by the secret door.

"Ask the sorcerer to eat with you tonight," Aladdin told Badr al-Budour. "Pretend to him that you now believe I am dead and so you are free to marry him. Invite him to dine with you this evening and secretly put this liquid into his drink. After that, leave the rest to me."

That evening, Badr al-Budour and the sorcerer sat down to dinner together. The sorcerer was in a good mood, for he felt that all his dreams had come true: he not only had the magic lamp but would soon have the beautiful Badr al-Budour as his wife.

The sorcerer ate well, celebrating his good fortune. By the time Aladdin entered the palace again and had gone to his wife's rooms, the sorcerer had drunk the liquid and was in a deep sleep.

Aladdin looked down at his sleeping enemy. Immediately he took out a long sword.

"Is he not dead already?" asked Badr al-Budour.

"There is only one way to be sure," answered Aladdin, and with one blow of the sword he killed the wicked sorcerer.

Aladdin then took the lamp from inside the sorcerer's robes. He rubbed it and immediately the genie was in front of him.

"Take this palace and put it down again in the place in which it was first built."

As soon as the palace had been moved back to the city in China, Aladdin and Badr al-Budour went to see her father. He had been weeping for his only daughter and could not believe his eyes when he saw her again, safe and sound. She immediately told her father about all that had happened.

The Sultan ordered that the city be decorated and that there should be a whole month of celebrations for the safe return of his daughter and her husband.

When, after several years, the Sultan died, Aladdin became the ruler of the city and was much loved by his people, and he and Badr al-Budour continued to live happily, surrounded by their children and their children's children.